North Carolina Nonprofit Law

A Concise Guide to Everything a Founder Needs to Know

Jacqueline D. Stanley
Attorney-at-Law

Copyright and Credits:

FIRST EDITION Print Book

Cover Designed By: Mica Roberts (djroberts@mindspring.com)

Table of Contents

Introduction

Nonprofits in North Carolina are governed by the North Carolina Nonprofit Corporation Act. My goal in writing this guide is to summarize the key provisions of the Act in order to allow you to familiarize yourself with them so you can focus on the work you created the organization to do. Do I think it is necessary for you to read the entire North Carolina Nonprofit Corporation Act? Absolutely not. It is written by lawyers for lawyers. And unless you are a lawyer, reading it will only create more confusion. You don't need to be an expert on nonprofit law, but you need to be an expert at doing whatever your nonprofit was created to do.

The Act is fairly comprehensive and includes regulations on everything from how to form or dissolve a nonprofit to board meeting notice and quorum requirements. However the Act provides broad latitude within which a nonprofit can operate. Unless something is specifically prohibited or mandated by the Act, then a nonprofit is free to act in accordance with its articles of incorporation, bylaws, or board authorization.

To get the most out of this guide my advice is that you read it once cover-to-cover and then ask each of your board members to do the same. Why? Because they share your responsibility for ensuring that your organization operates in accordance with the law. And I would also encourage you and your board to review this guide periodically to ensure your organization's ongoing compliance, and that you refer to it whenever you are confronted by one of the issues addressed in the guide.

It is important to note that this guide is not a substitute for legal representation or advice. Several places in the guide I have pointed to instances in which you should consult an attorney who has experience in North Carolina nonprofit law. However, any time you run into situations when you are unsure as to how to proceed and are unsure as to whether or not to consult an attorney, my advice would be to err on the side of caution and contact an attorney. My experience is that it is always easier and cheaper to avoid a legal problem than it is to resolve a legal problem.

Finally, let me close by congratulating you on your decision to start a nonprofit organization and to do work that will make a positive impact in the community in which you serve and a powerful difference in the lives of the people you help.

With respect and applause,

Jackie D. Stanley, ESQ.

Chapter One

Definition

The North Carolina Nonprofit Corporation Act defines a "nonprofit corporation" as *a corporation that has or will have no income or as a corporation that has or will have no income which is distributed to its members, directors or officers.*

Does that mean the founder of a nonprofit can't receive a salary from the organization he or she founded? No; the founder can be paid a salary for the services he or she renders on behalf of the organization. Typically, the founder of a nonprofit also serves as the executive director, president, or chief executive officer of the organization and is responsible for either conducting or overseeing the day-to-day operations of the organization. He or she can be paid for these services.

As a nonprofit founder you not only need to have a clear understanding of the definition of a nonprofit, but to ensure your organization remains in compliance with the Act you also must have a solid grasp on the key differences between a for-profit corporation and a nonprofit corporation. For-profit corporations are created and exist to benefit the private interests of the founder(s), the founder(s) family, or other entities controlled or designated by the founder(s). Nonprofits are created and exist to benefit public interests.

To further illustrate the difference between a for-profit corporation and a nonprofit corporation, consider this example:

Diane owns and operates "Diane's Dance School," which she incorporates as a for-profit corporation. Unless she has investors to whom she must answer, Diane can make all the decisions regarding the school's day-to-day operations. She can market to whomever she wants and charge whatever fees she deems are appropriate. If someone offers to buy her business Diane can sell it at whatever price she wants. And if at some point Diane needs to raise money in order to open a new location or to remodel her existing location, she can take on a partner or authorize the issuance of shares of stock.

If Diane wakes up one morning and decides it is time to hang up her tap shoes, she can close the doors of her business. She can also decide to change the name of her business to "Diane's Dance School and Donut Shop" because in addition to dance lessons she wants to sells donuts. Or, she can keep the name, stop teaching dance, and begin selling donuts exclusively.

Since Diane owns the business, she also owns any revenue or profits the business generates. And at her death, her business interest, assets and property can be passed on to her parents, spouse, children or whomever she designates.

However, if Diane had incorporated "Diane's Dance School" as a nonprofit corporation, the school would need to be governed by a board of directors. This means Diane will not be able to make any major decisions regarding the school or act on behalf of the organization without the board's prior knowledge and approval. So although Diane founded the organization, she would not have the authority to change its name or mission, or to sell or dissolve the organization.

Since nonprofits are strictly prohibited from issuing stock, when the school needs money it would either need to raise revenue through fundraising or by applying for grants or soliciting donations and sponsorships. At Diane's death, the nonprofit's assets or property would not be passed along to her parents, spouse, or children. It would be the board's responsibility to appoint or hire someone to take over whatever role Diane once held in the organization, and to decide how to move forward in a way that best serves the organization.

Chapter Two

Articles of Incorporation

The "articles of incorporation" is the document that is filed with the Secretary of State's office and that is used to formally create or incorporate a nonprofit corporation. You or your attorney can create the articles, or you can use the form provided by the Secretary of State.

The articles of incorporation <u>must</u> include the following information:

<u>Name of the Organization:</u> Whatever name you choose to list in the articles of incorporation is the "legal name" of the nonprofit and it is the name you should use on <u>all</u> legal documents thereafter. For example, if you use the name "Do Work That Matters Incorporated" on your articles of incorporation then it would not be appropriate for you to apply for your federal identification number with the name "Do Work That Matters Inc" or to use the name "Do Work That Matters" on your employment contracts.

<u>Purpose Clause:</u> If your nonprofit intends to seek 501(c)(3) tax exempt status then in order to meet the IRS requirements the following paragraph should be used as your purpose clause:

Said organization is organized exclusively for charitable, religious, educational, and scientific purposes, including for such purposes, the making of distributions to organizations that qualify as exempt organizations under Sections 501(c)(3) and 170(c)(2) of the Internal Revenue Code of 1986 (herein the "Code") (or the corresponding provisions of any future United States Internal Revenue Code.)

<u>Name and Street Address of the Registered Agent:</u> The registered agent is the person who is authorized to accept formal service of

process on behalf of the organization. In other words, if someone files legal action against the nonprofit this is the person to whom they are to send the court papers. Initially, the founder is the person who routinely serves as the registered agent. In the future, if it becomes necessary, the Secretary of State has a form that can be used to change the name and street address of the registered agent.

Mailing/Principal Address of the Organization: You can use a post office box as the nonprofit's mailing address. However, the principal office address must be a street address. The founder can use his or her home address as the mailing and principal address.

Name and Street Address of the Incorporator(s): The incorporator is the person(s) who actually files the articles of incorporation on behalf of the organization. The incorporator is usually either the founder, an attorney or some other person or entity retained to provide this service.

Dissolution Clause: The articles of incorporation must include a clause that outlines what will happen to the nonprofit's assets in the event the organization is dissolved. If your nonprofit intends to seek 501(c)(3) tax exempt status then in order to meet the IRS requirements the following paragraph should be used as your dissolution clause:

Upon the dissolution of the corporation, the Board of Directors shall, after paying or making provision for the payment of all of the liabilities of the corporation, dispose of all of the assets of the corporation exclusively for the purposes of the corporation in such manner, or to such organization or organizations organized and operated exclusively for religious, charitable, educational, scientific, or literary purposes as shall at the time qualify as an exempt organization or organizations under Section 501(c)(3) of Code as the Board of Directors shall determine, or to federal, state, or local governments to be used exclusively for public purposes. Any such assets not so disposed of shall be disposed of by the Superior Court of the county in which the principal office of the corporation is then located, exclusively for such purposes or to such purposes or to such organizations, such as the court shall determine, which are organized and operated exclusively for such purposes, or to such government for such purposes.

Members: You will also need to designate whether or not your organization has members. This is not a reference to board members. Membership organizations are nonprofits which allow or require people to join and offer specifically designated benefits and rights associated with membership. This may or may not include the right to vote on matters relating to the operation and governance of the organization. Typically the dues paid by members is the sole or primary revenue source for membership organizations. Examples of organizations with members include churches, unions, fraternities and sororities.

Effective Date: The articles of incorporation will be effective on the date they are filed with the Secretary of State unless you designate a different date.

Articles of Amendment

You may add, delete or change any of the provisions in your organization's articles of incorporation at any time it is deemed necessary by your board of directors. Of course, the additions, deletions or changes can't result in the removal of any of the information that is required by the Secretary of State or the IRS. For example, you can change the name of your registered agent but you can't change your articles of incorporation so that it no longer includes a registered agent.

Any amendment to the articles of incorporation must be approved by a majority vote of your board of directors. Prior to any board meeting in which a vote will be taken to amend the articles of

> BEST PRACTICE: Amending the articles of incorporation is a big deal. That's why some nonprofits impose even more stringent requirements than those required by the Act. Some organizations choose to require a larger percentage of affirmative votes to approve amendments. For example, although the Act only requires a majority vote, an organization may require an affirmative vote by seventy-five percent of their board members before any changes can be made to their articles of incorporation. Other nonprofits have decided that votes to amend their articles of incorporation will not be allowed until they consult with an attorney regarding the impact and necessity of the amendment.

incorporation, each board member must be given at least five days' written notice of the meeting. The written notice must state that the purpose of the meeting is to vote on a proposed amendment to the articles of incorporation and it must include a copy or a detailed summary of the proposed amendment.

Typically, there are only two instances when it is necessary for nonprofits to amend their articles of incorporation. The first is when an organization has filed its articles of incorporation and failed to include one or more of the necessary provisions needed to obtain a 501(c)(3) tax exemption, such as a failure to use the standard purpose or dissolution clause outlined above.

The second—and more common—instance when it is necessary for a nonprofit to amend its articles of incorporation is when it decides to change its name. I have seen many situations when the founder selects a name that only makes sense to him or her and then later on as the organization grows, the board decides that it is in the nonprofit's best interest to change its name.

Impact of Amendments on Legal Action

An amendment to your articles of incorporation will not impact any pending legal action you may have filed or that may have been filed against your organization. For example, let's say the legal name of your organization is Do Work That Matters Inc. and your landlord files a lawsuit against you for past due rent. Changing the name of the organization to Doing Important Work That Really Matters Inc. will not stop the pending lawsuit by your landlord from moving forward under the original name of the organization.

Chapter Three

Bylaws

The North Carolina Nonprofit Corporation Act defines "bylaws" as *the written document that outlines the rules and regulations that govern the management of a nonprofit's affairs.* Any document that meets this definition will be deemed to be the organization's bylaws although they may choose to refer to this document by another name. For example, some nonprofits use the word "charter" instead of the word "bylaws" when referring to their governing document.

Bylaws are considered to be a living and breathing document that changes, expands, and contracts as needed to further the organization's mission. It is for this reason that an organization may amend its bylaws as needed. An amendment to the bylaws requires an affirmative vote by a majority of board members. Each board member must be given at least five days' written notice of any meeting in which a vote will be taken to amend the bylaws. The written notice must state that the purpose of the meeting is to vote on a proposed amendment to the bylaws and it must include a copy or a detailed summary of the proposed amendment.

BEST PRACTICE: The North Carolina Nonprofit Corporation Act states that nonprofits must have bylaws, but it does not dictate the specific provisions that must be included in them. However, that does not mean you should include whatever you want. Sometimes a nonprofit founder is so concerned that he or she will lose control of the organization he or she worked hard to create, that he or she will draft bylaws that contain provisions essentially making him or her "supreme ruler for life" of the organization. This is a huge mistake. If you apply for 501(c)(3) tax exempt status you will be required to submit a copy of your bylaws as part of the application package. And if your bylaws give you as the founder free reign to do whatever you want and contains provisions stripping the board of directors of any meaningful authority to oversee or manage the organization, the IRS may deny your request for tax exemption. If you apply for grants and sponsorships, many of them will also require you to submit a copy of your bylaws as part of the application package, and if your bylaws are poorly drafted it may hurt your chances of being awarded a grant or sponsorship.

12 Key Provisions That Should Be Included in Your Bylaws

1. The legal name of the organization
2. Principal office address of the organization
3. Rules governing the election and removal of board members
4. Rules governing the time and location of board meetings
5. Rules regarding the election and removal of officers
6. Fiscal procedures and policies (e.g., contracts, loans, checks, and deposits)
7. Policies regarding the maintenance of corporate books and accounting records
8. Fiscal year designation
9. Rules governing the creation of committee(s)
10. Rules governing the election and removal of committee members
11. Rules regarding indemnification
12. Rules regarding the repeal or amendment of the bylaws

BEST PRACTICE: Properly drafted bylaws are the cornerstone of any successful nonprofit organization. It is imperative that you put as much time and attention in creating and crafting your bylaws as you put into creating and starting your nonprofit. They should be drafted to meet the specific needs and operation of your organization. That's why it is not a good idea to simply download sample bylaws from the internet, insert your organization's name and adopt them as your own. You should consider consulting an experienced nonprofit attorney about drafting your organization's bylaws or reviewing the bylaws you create.

Chapter Four

Board of Directors

The North Carolina Nonprofit Corporation Act defines the "board of directors" as *the group of natural persons vested by the corporation with the management of its affairs whether or not the group is designated as directors in the articles of incorporation or bylaws.* Nonprofits must have a board of directors and all corporate powers must be exercised by or under their authority.

Here is a list of the corporate powers that only the board of directors has the power to exercise:

- Amend the articles of incorporation or bylaws.
- Fill board vacancies.
- Appoint the officers (e.g., chair, vice chair, secretary, or treasurer).
- Remove board members elected by the board (this requires a majority vote unless a higher percentage is required by the bylaws).
- Remove officers.
- Create or dissolve board committees.
- Fix the compensation of board members.
- Authorize distributions.

It's important to note that your board members do not have to reside in the state of North Carolina. And unless you specify otherwise in your articles of incorporation or bylaws, the term of each member shall be one year. Board members may serve successive terms and may resign at any time for any reason.

> BEST PRACTICE: North Carolina nonprofits are only required to have one board member. However, if you plan to apply for 501(c)(3) tax exempt status you will need to have at least three. I advise my clients that they should have at least three board members or any odd number greater than three. An odd number of board members will help to avoid voting deadlocks.

Chapter Five

Board Officers

There is no requirement that a nonprofit board have officers. Your bylaws may state that your nonprofit board will not have any officers. Or, your board can have whatever officers that are designated in your bylaws or appointed by the board of directors.

> BEST PRACTICE: The board of a nonprofit that plans to seek 501(c)(3) tax exempt status should have at least these three officers: a president, a treasurer, and a secretary. The president presides over the board meetings, the treasurer maintains the financial records, and a secretary has the responsibility and authority to maintain and authenticate the records of the corporation. The officers shall have whatever specific duties and authority designated by the bylaws, or established by the board of directors.

Please note that the same person can serve dual roles on the board. But, the law is clear that one person cannot act in more than one role when the approval of two or more officers is required. For example, the same person can serve as both the secretary and the treasurer. However, if the bylaws require the signature of two officers on checks, he or she cannot sign the check twice in both capacities. A different officer will need to provide the second signature.

Resignation and Removal

Officers may resign at any time for any reason. And the board of directors may remove an officer at any time for any reason.

Chapter Six

Board Committees

There is no requirement that a nonprofit board have committees. Your bylaws can specifically prohibit the creation of committees. Or, your bylaws may allow the board to create one or more committees of the board and appoint board members to serve on them. Committees will consist of two or more board members who serve at the pleasure of the board. Three examples of the types of committees your nonprofit board might create include an executive committee, finance committee, or fundraising committee.

The creation of a committee or the appointment of board members to serve on a committee must be approved by an affirmative vote of the majority of the board members. Again, your bylaws or articles of incorporation may require a number of affirmative votes that is greater than a majority. For example, let's say your nonprofit has 13 board members. Seven affirmative votes would constitute a majority, but your bylaws or articles of incorporation could require nine affirmative votes to create or appoint a member to serve on a committee. But it could not require only five affirmative votes because that would be less than a majority vote.

Committees and committee members are required to follow all of the same rules regarding meetings, notice, quorum, and voting that the full board of directors must follow. And committees and committee members may exercise board authority only to the extent allowed by the board, the bylaws, or the articles of incorporation.

Four Things Board Committees and Committee Members Are Prohibited From Doing

Board committees are designed to support the board and are not intended to act as the full board of directors. That is why to ensure a committee of three or four board members does not usurp the power of the full board, committees and committee members are specifically prohibited from doing any of the following:

- Authorizing distributions (see Chapter 15).
- Selling, pledging or transferring all or substantially all of the nonprofit's assets or property.
- Electing, appointing or removing board members, or filling the vacancies on the board or any of its committees.
- Adopting, amending, or repealing the articles of incorporation or bylaws.

Chapter Seven

Standards of Conduct for Board Members

The North Carolina Nonprofit Corporation Act has established a standard of conduct for anyone serving on the board of a nonprofit. It states that a board member shall discharge his or her duties as a director, including his or her duties as a member of a committee as follows:

- **In good faith: this means board members must act openly, honestly, and without any design or intention to be deceptive.** A board member acts in bad faith when he or she does something that he or she knows is inappropriate, illegal, or unauthorized by the organization's articles of incorporation, bylaws or other members of the board.

- **With the care that an ordinarily prudent person in a like position would exercise under similar circumstances.** I refer to this as the "common sense" clause. For example, if a board member discovers that another board member is stealing from the organization, then most people would agree that it makes "common sense" that he or she should immediately report this to the full board.

- **In a manner the board member reasonably believes to be in the best interest of the organization.** The "best interest of the organization" should be the polar star that guides board members. Board members should have no allegiance to the founder of the nonprofit or the other members of the board. His or her only allegiance should be to the organization and ensuring that its activities and affairs are legally operated and effectively managed in a manner that will allow it to fulfill the purpose for which it was created.

In discharging his or her duties, a board member may rely on the information, opinions, reports or statements, including financial statements and other financial data, if prepared or presented by:

- **One or more officers or employees of the organization whom the board member reasonably believes to be reliable and competent in the matters presented**. It is reasonable to believe that a financial report prepared by an accountant is reliable. However, it is not reasonable to believe that an accounting report prepared by someone you know who is not an accountant is reliable.

- **Legal counsel, public accountants, or other persons as to matters the board member reasonably believes are within their professional or expert competence.** It is reasonable to believe that a legal opinion prepared by a licensed attorney is reliable. It is not reasonable to believe that a legal opinion prepared by an attorney you know has been disbarred is reliable.

- **A committee of the board of which he or she is not a member, if the board member reasonably believes the committee merits confidence.** It is reasonable to believe that a financial report presented by the financial committee is reliable. It is not reasonable to believe a report presented by the financial committee is reliable if you know the committee does not have access to the nonprofit's financial records.

Important Note: As long as a board member acts in accordance with the above standard of conduct, he or she cannot be held liable for any actions he or she takes or fails to take with regard to the organization. However, if a board member has actual knowledge of misconduct then he or she cannot hide behind the fact that he or she reasonably relied on information provided by one of the above three sources. For example, if a board member knows the organization's treasurer has embezzled funds from the organization, he or she can't use the fact that an audit by a CPA firm did not reveal the embezzlement as justification for his or her failure to report the embezzlement to the proper authorities.

Chapter Eight

Conflict of Interest Transactions

A conflict of interest transaction arises in situations in which there is a financial transaction between a nonprofit organization and an entity in which one or more of its board members has either a direct or indirect interest.

Here are three examples of conflict of interest transactions:

- **Transactions between a nonprofit organization and a board member.**
  Example: Your organization leases office space from one of your board members.
- **Transactions between a nonprofit organization and any business or entity in which a board member is a partner or has a significant financial interest.**
  Example: Your organization hires a law firm in which one of your board members is a partner.
- **Transactions between a nonprofit organization and any organization in which one of its board members also serves as a board member, director, officer or trustee.**
  Example: You have a board member who serves on the board of another nonprofit organization and your organization buys property from that organization.

The North Carolina Nonprofit Corporation Act does <u>not</u> prohibit conflict of interest transactions in the following two instances:

- The nature of the conflict was disclosed to the board of directors and it authorized, approved or ratified the transaction. A conflict of interest transaction is authorized, approved, or ratified if it receives the affirmative vote of a majority of the members of the board who have no direct or indirect interest in the transaction. A single board member cannot authorize, approve, or ratify a conflict of interest transaction.

- The transaction was fair to the nonprofit organization.

> BEST PRACTICE: An organization's articles of incorporation or bylaws can prohibit or establish more stringent restrictions for conflict of interest transactions. And if a nonprofit organization plans to obtain 501(c)(3) tax exempt status it must adopt policies and procedures to protect the organization's interest when it is contemplating entering into these type of transactions.

Banned Activities

The following transactions are strictly prohibited by the North Carolina Nonprofit Corporation Act:

- A nonprofit organization cannot loan money to a board member, director or officer.
- A nonprofit organization cannot serve as the guarantor of a loan made to a board member, director or officer.

What happens if a board member votes or assents to authorize one of the above banned activities? If it is determined that the board member breached the standard of conduct outlined in Chapter Seven, he or she could be forced to repay the money loaned or lost plus interest back to the organization. There is a three-year statute of limitations on the filing of any legal action against a board member by an organization seeking reimbursement in this situation.

Chapter Nine

Board Meetings

The North Carolina Nonprofit Corporation Act does not mandate when or where your board meetings should take place. Although it does provide that your organizational, regular or special meetings can take place in or outside the state of North Carolina.

Organizational Meeting

At some point soon after you receive a filed copy of your articles of incorporation, you should convene an organizational meeting for the purpose of doing the following two things:

- Adopting bylaws
- Appointing or electing board members

Important Note: The bylaws can be formally adopted and the board members can be elected or appointed without an organizational meeting by the written consent of the incorporators. The document containing the incorporators consent should be filed and maintained as part of the organization's official records.

Regular Meetings

Your bylaws should include the frequency of regular board meetings. Typically organizations have regular monthly, bi-monthly, or yearly board meetings. You are not required to send board members notice of regular meetings.

Your board meetings can take place in a physical location or they can be conducted via telephone, video conference, or any other electronic means that allows all board members to hear all of the other board members simultaneously during the meeting.

Assuming there is no specific prohibition in your bylaws or articles of incorporation, board members can take action without a board meeting as long as there is a written record of the action that includes the signed consent of all members of the board. The written record must be filed and maintained as part of your organization's official records.

Special Meetings

Twenty percent of your board members or the presiding officer of your board of directors can call or schedule a special meeting of your board. Board members must be given at least five days' notice of a special meeting. Notice of a special meeting must be sent by the same medium by which you normally communicate with your board members.

Board members may waive the right to receive notice of a special meeting. The waiver must be in writing and filed along with the minutes of the meeting. A board member who attends or participates in a special meeting waives the notice requirement unless, immediately upon arrival, he or she objects to holding the special meeting.

Quorum

A "quorum" is the minimum number of board members required to be present at a board meeting in order for the board to have authority to conduct business. The North Carolina Nonprofit Corporation Act defines a quorum as *a majority of the directors in office immediately before a meeting begins*.

For example, if your board consists of nine board members, then at least five members must be present at board meetings in order to have the quorum needed to conduct business.

Your bylaws or articles of incorporation may change the quorum requirement however it cannot authorize a quorum of fewer than one-third of your board members.

For example, if your board consists of nine board members, your bylaws can authorize a quorum of less than a majority of the board members but it could not authorize a quorum of fewer than three board members.

Voting

If a board member is present at a meeting when a decision is made or an action is taken on behalf of the organization then it will be assumed that he or she agreed to the decision or the action that was taken unless:

- At the beginning of the meeting or immediately upon his or her arrival, he or she objects to holding the meeting or to conducting business.
- He or she objects to the decision or the action being taken and his or her objection is recorded in the minutes.
- He or she abstains from voting on the decision or action being taken and his or her abstention is recorded in the minutes.
- He or she submits a written notice of his or her objection or abstention to the presiding officer of the board meeting before the meeting is adjourned or he or she sends a written notice of his or her objection or abstention to the organization immediately after the meeting is adjourned.

Chapter Ten

Records and Reports

The North Carolina Nonprofit Corporation Act mandates that nonprofit organizations maintain the following documents as part of their permanent records:

- The minutes of all board meetings.
- A record of all actions taken by the board of directors without a board meeting.
- A record of all actions taken by board committees in place of the board of directors on behalf of the organization.

Your records must be maintained in written form or in any other form that can be quickly converted into written form.

> BEST PRACTICE: Nonprofit organizations are also required to maintain appropriate accounting records. You should consult an accountant with experience in helping nonprofits about how to create and maintain your accounting records.

Your organization must also maintain a copy of the following records at your principal office:

- Your articles of incorporation and all amendments to them currently in effect.
- Your bylaws or restated bylaws and all amendments to them currently in effect.
- Resolutions adopted by your board of directors relating to the number, duties, and qualifications of your board members.

- A list of the names and business and home addresses of your current board members and officers.

Chapter Eleven

Indemnification

"Indemnification" is the process by which an organization can protect its board members from lawsuits or other legal action by agreeing to pay or reimburse any legal or other reasonable expenses they incur as a result of a civil or criminal proceeding filed against them because they are or were members of the organization's board of directors.

In order to allow nonprofit organizations the ability to attract qualified and competent people to serve on their board of directors, the North Carolina Nonprofit Corporation Act grants nonprofit organizations the authority to indemnify board members in the following situations:

- The board member seeking indemnification acted in "good faith."
- The board member, acting in his or her official capacity, was reasonable in believing his or her conduct was in the organization's best interests.
- The board member, not acting in his or her official capacity, was reasonable in believing his or her conduct was not opposed to the organization's best interest.
- The board member had no reason to believe his or her conduct was unlawful.

There are certain situations in which a nonprofit organization can not indemnify a board member. They are as follows:

- In a legal proceeding in which a board member is held liable to the nonprofit organization.

- In a legal proceeding in which it is alleged that the board member was held liable for receiving an improper personal benefit.

The determination as to whether an organization should indemnify or not indemnify a board member in a particular situation can be made in one of the following ways:

- A majority vote of the board members not involved in the legal proceeding; or
- If a quorum cannot be obtained, then by a majority vote of a committee duly designated by the board of directors that consists of two or more board members that are not a party to the legal proceeding; or
- The board of directors can retain special legal counsel to make the determination.

Important Note: Your organization's bylaws or articles of incorporation can establish indemnification policies and procedures that are consistent with the mandates outlined above.

BEST PRACTICE: Although it is not required, your organization should purchase and maintain indemnification insurance on behalf of your board members. If your organization decides not to purchase or maintain indemnification insurance, it may be difficult for your organization to attract high quality and qualified board members. The insurance agent that handles your car, life, or homeowner's insurance may be a good resource for finding an agency from which your organization can obtain indemnification insurance.

Chapter Twelve

Immunity

A person serving as a board member of a nonprofit organization is immune from civil liability for personally paying any monetary damages, except to the extent covered by insurance, for any act or failure to act arising out of his or her service as a board member.

There are a few exceptions to this rule. Board members in the following situations are not immune from personally paying monetary damages:

- A board member who is paid for serving on the board.
- A board member who is not acting within the scope of his or her official duties.
- A board member who is not acting in good faith.
- A board member who commits gross negligence or willful or wanton misconduct in the damage or injury.
- A board member who derives an improper personal financial benefit from the transaction that is the subject of the civil lawsuit.
- The civil liability arises from the operation of a motor vehicle.
- A board member is a defendant in an action brought for unlawful loans or distributions.

The immunity granted by the North Carolina Nonprofit Corporation Act may be limited or eliminated by a provision in the organization's articles of incorporation or bylaws, but only with respect to acts or omissions occurring on or after the effective date of such provision.

Important Note: The immunity granted by the North Carolina Nonprofit Corporation Act only applies to individual board members; it does not apply to the organization. For example, let's say someone sues Good Deeds Inc. and one of its board members for something the board member did or did not do. The most the board member will have to pay is the amount covered by the insurance. The organization, on the other hand, may be forced to pay the full amount of the monetary damages.

Chapter Thirteen

Merger

A nonprofit organization may merge into another nonprofit organization. For example, Happy People Inc. and Healthy People Inc. could merge into one another and become Happy and Healthy People Inc. Mergers between two or more organizations must be approved by an affirmative vote of a majority of the board members of each organization.

Board members must be given at least five days' written notice of any meeting at which approval of a proposed plan of merger is being addressed. The notice must clearly state that the purpose of the meeting is to vote on a proposed plan of merger and must include a copy of the proposed plan.

The North Carolina Nonprofit Corporation Act places the following restrictions on mergers:

- A North Carolina charitable or religious organization may merge with another North Carolina charitable or religious organization.
- A North Carolina charitable or religious organization may only merge with a charitable or religious organization that is incorporated outside the state of North Carolina if that organization would qualify as charitable or religious corporation if it were incorporated in North Carolina.
- A North Carolina charitable or religious organization may only merge with another organization that is not a charitable or religious organization, if the organization that survives the merger continues to be a charitable or religious organization.

A merger does not officially take effect until the surviving organization files articles of merger with the Secretary of State.

BEST PRACTICE: You should consult an attorney prior to merging with another organization.

Chapter Fourteen

Transfer of Assets

A transfer of assets includes any of the following transactions: sale, lease, exchange, mortgage, pledge, or any other means of encumbering property. A nonprofit organization may transfer assets with the approval of a majority of its board members.

Notice Requirement

There are two situations in which board members must be given five days' written notice of any meetings at which board authorization to transfer assets will be considered:

- The transfer of assets is outside the course of the organization's regular course of activities.
- The transfer of assets includes the disposition of all or a substantial portion of the organization's assets or property.

The notice must clearly state that the purpose of the meeting is to vote on the transfer of all or a substantial portion of the organization's property or assets and it must include a detailed description of the proposed transfers.

BEST PRACTICE: There are instances in which a charitable or religious organization will also need to give notice to the Attorney General of North Carolina prior to the transfer of all or a substantial portion of its assets. You should consult an attorney prior to transferring all or substantial portion of your organization's assets.

Chapter Fifteen

Distributions

The North Carolina Nonprofit Corporation Act defines a "distribution" as *a direct or indirect transfer of money or other property to or for the benefit of a board member or officer*. Non-profits may pay reasonable amounts to its members, directors, or officers for services rendered. An organization's bylaws may prohibit distributions or establish the limits of amounts paid to board members. Distributions must be approved by a majority of board members.

Important Note: A non-profit organization may also make distributions to any entity that is exempt under section 501(c)(3) of the Internal Revenue Code of 1986 or any successor section. It may also make distributions to any entity that is organized exclusively for one or more of the purposes specified in section 501(c)(3) of the Internal Revenue Code of 1986 or any successor section, and that upon dissolution shall distribute its assets to a charitable or religious corporation, the United States, a state, or an entity that is exempt under section 501(c)(3) of the Internal Revenue Code of 1986 or any successor section.

A nonprofit organization is prohibited from making distributions in following two situations:

- As a result of the distribution the organization will no longer be able to pay its bills as they become due; or
- As a result of the distribution the organization's liabilities will exceed its total assets.

Chapter Sixteen

Dissolution

Voluntary Dissolution Prior to Commencement of Activities

A nonprofit that has not yet begun operations or acquired any assets or property may be dissolved by a majority vote of its board members. If the nonprofit has not yet appointed board members then a majority of its incorporators can vote to dissolve the organization.

Once the board of directors or incorporators authorize the dissolution, the nonprofit must file Articles of Dissolution with the Secretary of State.

Voluntary Dissolution After the Commencement of Activities

The board of directors of a nonprofit that has begun operating or that has acquired assets or property may authorize a board meeting to develop a proposed plan for dissolving the organization. Unless the bylaws or board of directors require a higher percentage, the plan of dissolution must be approved by a majority of board members.

Board members must be given at least five days' written notice of any meeting at which approval of a proposed plan of dissolution is being addressed. The notice must clearly state that the purpose of the meeting is to vote on a proposed plan of dissolution and must include a copy of the proposed plan of dissolution.

Plan of Dissolution

A nonprofit's plan of dissolution must include the means by which all of its debts or other financial obligations will be paid or discharged. Any of its remaining assets or property must be distributed as follows:

- Any assets or property the nonprofit agreed to return to the grantor upon dissolution shall be returned to them in accordance with their agreement.
- Other assets, if any, of a charitable or religious corporation shall, subject to the articles of incorporation or bylaws, be transferred or conveyed to one or more of the following: the United States, a state, a charitable or religious corporation, or a person that is exempt under section 501(c)(3) of the Internal Revenue Code of 1986 or any successor section.

Effect of Dissolution

After the effective date of dissolution, a nonprofit may no longer engage in its normal activities and operations. It can only conduct the business and activities needed to implement its plan of dissolution and close out its financial affairs. Closing out its financial affairs includes sending written notice of its dissolution to its creditors or other entities who may have claims against them. A nonprofit may also publish notice of its dissolution in a newspaper and request that anyone with claims submit the claims as outlined in the notice.

As a general rule, any legal claims filed against a nonprofit after the date of dissolution will be barred from collection or prosecution. However, there are three key exceptions to this rule. Dissolution will not bar or protect a nonprofit from the following claims:

- Legal claims alleging the liability of the nonprofit.
- Legal proceedings or actions to establish the liability of the nonprofit.
- Legal proceedings initiated to enforce or recover any judgment(s) already entered against the nonprofit.

Revocation of Dissolution

A nonprofit may revoke its dissolution within 120 days of the effective date of the dissolution. The revocation of dissolution must be authorized by the same manner as the dissolution was authorized. The revocation of dissolution shall not be effective until the Articles of Revocation of Dissolution are filed the Secretary of State.

When the revocation of dissolution is effective, it relates back to and takes effect as of the effective date of the dissolution and the nonprofit may resume its activities as if dissolution had never occurred.

Administrative Dissolution

A nonprofit may be administratively dissolved by the Secretary of State in the following situations:

- The nonprofit does not pay penalties, fees, or other payments requested by the Secretary of State within 60 days after they are due.
- The nonprofit is without a registered agent or registered office in North Carolina for 60 days or more.
- The nonprofit fails to notify the Secretary of State within 60 days that its registered agent or registered office has been changed, that its registered agent has resigned, or that its registered office has been discontinued.
- The period of duration stated in the nonprofit's articles of incorporation expires.
- The nonprofit knowingly fails or refuses to answer truthfully and fully inquiries made by the Secretary of State.
- The nonprofit fails to designate the address of its principal office with the Secretary of State or does not notify the Secretary of State within 60 days that the principal office has changed.

Reinstatement Following Administrative Dissolution

A nonprofit that has been administratively dissolved may apply to the Secretary of State for reinstatement. If the reinstatement is allowed, it relates back to and takes effect as of the effective date of the administrative dissolution and the nonprofit may resume carrying on its activities as if the administrative dissolution had never occurred.

Important Note: If the Secretary of State denies a nonprofit's request for reinstatement it may appeal the denial to the Superior Court of Wake County within 30 days after it receives the notice of denial.

Judicial Dissolution

The Superior Court may dissolve a nonprofit in a legal proceeding initiated by any of the following, with important qualifications:

The North Carolina Attorney General's Office, if it is established that:

- The nonprofit obtained its articles of incorporation through fraud.
- The nonprofit after receiving written notice by the Attorney General continues to exceed or abuse the authority conferred upon it by the laws of North Carolina.

A Board Member, if it is established that:

- The board of directors is deadlocked in the management of the nonprofit's affairs.
- The board of directors or those in control of the nonprofit have acted, are acting, or will act in a manner that is illegal, oppressive, or fraudulent.
- The nonprofit's assets are being misapplied or wasted.

- The nonprofit is no longer able to carry out the purpose for which it was created.

A Creditor, if it is established that:

- The creditor's claim has been reduced to judgment and execution on the judgment has been returned unsatisfied.
- The nonprofit has admitted in writing that the creditor's claim is due and owing and the nonprofit is insolvent.

The Nonprofit itself, if it is established that:

- The nonprofit wishes to have its voluntary dissolution proceed under the supervision of the court.

Important Note: Prior to dissolving a nonprofit, the Superior Court will consider whether there are reasonable alternatives to dissolution and whether the dissolution is in the best interest of the public.

APPENDIX:

North Carolina Nonprofit Corporation Act

Best Practice Checklist

Articles of Incorporation

- ☐ Maintain a copy of your articles of incorporation and any amendments at your principal office.
- ☐ Only use the legal name listed on your articles of incorporation on legal documents.
- ☐ Review your articles of incorporation regularly and at any time there is a change in your registered agent(s) name or address or a change in your principal office or mailing address file the updated information with the Secretary of State.

Bylaws

- ☐ Maintain a copy of your bylaws and any amendments at your principal office.
- ☐ Review and refer to your bylaws on a regular basis to ensure compliance.

Board Meetings

☐ Verify that you have a quorum present prior to the commencement of each board meeting.

☐ Record and maintain a copy of the board meeting minutes as part of your permanent records.

☐ Schedule and conduct your regular board meetings as outlined in your bylaws.

☐ Give board members at least <u>five days'</u> notice of any meeting at which any of the following actions will be considered:

    ☐ Amending articles of incorporation

    ☐ Amending bylaws

    ☐ Transferring assets outside normal course of business

    ☐ Merging with another organization

    ☐ Calling a special meeting

    ☐ Dissolving the organization

Board of Directors

☐ Make sure the following actions receive board authorization and approval and that their authorization and approval is recorded in the minutes:

    ☐ Amend the articles of incorporation or bylaws

    ☐ Fill board vacancies

    ☐ Appoint the officers (e.g., chair, vice chair, secretary or treasurer)

    ☐ Remove any board members elected by the board (Requires a majority vote unless a higher percentage is required by the bylaws.)

- ☐ Remove any officers
- ☐ Create or dissolve board committees
- ☐ Fix the compensation of board members
- ☐ Authorize distributions

☐ Maintain a record of all actions taken by the board without a meeting as part of your permanent records.

☐ Maintain a record of all actions taken by board committees in the place of the board of directors on behalf of the organization.

☐ Make sure existing and new board members are aware of their obligation to discharge his or her duties as a board member as follows:

- ☐ In good faith
- ☐ With the care an ordinarily prudent person in a like position would exercise under similar circumstances
- ☐ In a manner the board member reasonably believes to be in the best interest of the organization

☐ Maintain any resolutions adopted by your board of directors relating to the number, duties and qualifications of your board members at your principal office.

☐ Maintain a list of the names and business and home addresses of your current board members and officers at your principal office.

Fiscal Policies and Procedures

☐ Consult with an accountant to help you set up and maintain appropriate accounting records.

☐ Make sure all conflict of interest transactions are disclosed to the board of directors and they are authorized, approved or ratified by the board.

☐ Make sure all conflict of interest transactions are fair to the nonprofit.

Legal Consultation

☐ Consult a nonprofit attorney prior to taking these actions:

    ☐ Amending articles of incorporation

    ☐ Merging with another organization

    ☐ Transferring a substantial portion of your assets outside the normal course of business

    ☐ Authorizing distributions that will render the organization insolvent

    ☐ Dissolving the organization

    ☐ Authorizing a conflict of interest transaction where there is a question about whether it is in the organization's best interest

☐ Consult a nonprofit attorney in the following situations:

    ☐ You receive notice of administrative or judicial dissolution

    ☐ Your organization is served with legal papers

    ☐ One of your board members is served with legal papers

    ☐ You suspect a board member of breaching standards of conduct

    ☐ A board member makes a claim for indemnification

About the Author

Jackie Stanley is a graduate of Wake Forest University Law School (1990). She has co-authored and authored 11 books including *How to Start a Business in North Carolina.* She has taught classes, seminars and workshops at Guilford College, Wake Technical Community College and several other colleges throughout the state. Her law practice includes helping nonprofits obtain their 501(c)(3) tax exemption. And she proudly serves on the board of the Women's Resource Center in Greensboro, North Carolina.

Jackie is currently working on a series of books that will offer nonprofit founders the advice and assurance they need to start, manage and grow organizations that do work that matters. This is the first book in the series.

Jackie would love to hear what you think about this book as well as suggestions on other topics you think should be included in the series.

Here's how you can connect with Jackie:

Web: www.DoWorkThatMatters.org
Email: attorneyjackie@DoWorkThatMatters.org
Twitter: @attorneyjackie

Made in the USA
Charleston, SC
23 March 2014